D0914424

GREAT MOMENTS IN AMERICAN HISTORY

Life with the Comanches

The Kidnapping of Cynthia Ann Parker

Nancy Golden

rosen central
Primary Source™

The Rosen Publishing Group, Inc., New York

Published in 2004 by The Rosen Publishing Group, Inc.
29 East 21st Street, New York, NY 10010

Editor: Eric Fein
Book Design: Daniel Hosek
Photo researcher: Rebecca Anguin-Cohen

Photo Credits: Cover (left), title page, p. 10 University of Michigan Museum of Art/The Bridgeman
Art Library; cover (right) illustration © Debra Wainwright/The Rosen Publishing Group; pp. 6
(CN 00873), 22 (CN 04515) Center for American History, UT - Austin; pp. 14, 18 Smithsonian
American Art Museum, Washington, DC/ Art Resource, NY; p. 29 Lawrence T. Jones, III collection,
Austin, Texas; p. 30 (X-32238) Denver Public Library, Western History Collection; pp. 31, 32
Western History Collection, University of Oklahoma

First Edition

Library of Congress Cataloging-in-Publication Data

Golden, Nancy.
    Life with the Comanches : the kidnapping of Cynthia Ann Parker / Nancy
Golden.—1st ed.
    p. cm. — (Great moments in American history)
    Summary: Profiles Cynthia Ann Parker, who was captured in 1836 at the
age of nine and lived as a Comanche for more than twenty years.
    ISBN 0-8239-4344-5 (lib. bdg.)
    1. Parker, Cynthia Ann, 1827?-1864—Juvenile literature. 2. Comanche
Indians—Social life and customs--Juvenile literature. 3. Indian
captivities—Texas—Juvenile literature. 4. Texas—Biography—Juvenile
literature. [1. Parker, Cynthia Ann, 1827?-1864. 2. Comanche
Indians—Biography. 3. Indians of North America—Texas—Biography. 4.
Indian captivities—Texas. 5. Women—Biography.] I. Title. II. Series.

E99.C85P38273 2004
976.4004'9745—dc21

2003003922

Manufactured in the United States of America

Contents

Preface

The 1800s was a time of great growth in America. Thousands of pioneers traveled west across the country to find a better way of life. However, these pioneers were not moving to empty lands. Native American tribes, such as the Comanches, had been living on these lands for many years. Once the settlers moved in, life changed for the Native Americans.

The settlers took over the land. They killed the buffalo that the Native Americans used for food, clothing, and shelter. The Native Americans became angry at the settlers. Fighting between them broke out in many places. The Native Americans and the settlers raided each other's homes.

In 1833, the Parker family traveled west from Illinois to settle in Texas. They were looking for land on which to settle and set up their church. The oldest member of the Parker family was

called Elder John. He had moved with his wife, children, and grandchildren. They settled in eastern Texas.

Elder John along with three of his sons, James, Benjamin, and Silas built houses for the family. Around the houses, they built a high fence for protection. They called their new home Fort Parker.

Silas and his wife Lucy Parker had four children: John, Silas Jr., Orlena, and Cynthia Ann. Frontier life was hard for both adults and children. However, the Parker family was happy in their new homes. Unfortunately, life was about to change for the family—especially for young Cynthia Ann. Cynthia Ann would be caught in the middle of two warring cultures, the Native Americans and the white settlers. She would be torn not once but twice from the families she loved.

Her story begins on a May morning in 1836....

Fort Parker was built between 1833 and 1835. Today, a re-creation of the fort is used to teach people what pioneer life was like in Texas in the 1800s.

Chapter One

CAPTURED!

The sun was shining brightly. My brother, John, and I were playing outside Fort Parker. I was nine years old and John was six. Usually the gates to our fort are kept closed, and we stayed inside. "To keep us safe," said Mama. I know what we're keeping safe from: American Indians. I hear the grown-ups talking about Indians all the time. No one had seen any Indians in a while, so the gates had been left open. Inside the gates, my mother and the other women gathered to do their chores. It was a day much like all the other days since we came here to Texas.

Suddenly, I heard a noise. I looked up and saw a big cloud of dust about a half a mile away. "What is it, Cynthia Ann?" John asked.

Before I could answer him, I heard someone cry, "Indians! Indians!" There were hundreds of Indians riding toward our fort! We didn't know what to do. Everyone started running around in a panic.

"They have a white flag," I heard Mama say. I knew that a white flag was a sign of peace and friendship, but everyone was acting so scared!

My Uncle Ben went out to see what they wanted. Uncle Ben came back into the fort, and I heard him say that the Indians just wanted meat. Maybe they were hungry, just like we get sometimes. Yet Uncle Ben looked worried. He whispered something to Mama. I could tell something was wrong.

Uncle Ben went back out to talk to the Indians. All the women started grabbing the children and quickly taking us to the back of the fort. I heard yelling. It came from Uncle Ben. He was telling us to run. The Indians were making loud whooping noises. They came inside the fort.

We ran as fast as we could toward the back of the fort. There was so much dust I could barely see. I tried to keep close to my mother, but the Indians were all around. They were circling us on their horses.

"Don't hurt my babies," Mama cried to the Indians. She was holding us so tightly I could barely breathe. The Indians were pointing at John and me. They wanted Mama to give us to them! I know she didn't want to, but they threatened her with a tomahawk.

She put each of us up on a horse with an Indian. I wanted to scream, but nothing came out of my mouth. The horse took off quickly. As I turned around, I could see Mama crying.

I could think only of one thing: *Would I ever see my family again?*

Settlers, such as the ones pictured on the wagon, were often attacked by Native Americans. The Native Americans were angry because the settlers were driving them from their lands.

Chapter Two

MY LIFE HAS CHANGED

We rode for a long time until we came upon another group of Indians. When we stopped, John and I were thrown onto the ground. John crawled over to me and started to cry. I put my arms around him and said, "Don't worry, John. If we behave, they won't hurt us." I was wrong.

The Indians tied our hands and legs with some kind of rope. They hit me and then they hit John. "Don't hit my brother!" I yelled. They pushed me down and hit me again.

"I want my mama and papa!" John kept crying. I could see that his crying was making the Indians angry. I tried to keep him quiet. One of the Indians came up and grabbed John. I tried to stop him, but I couldn't. The Indian put John up on a

horse and rode away. *Where is he taking him?* I wondered. I was tired and upset. I cried myself to sleep.

When I woke up, I couldn't remember where I was. I was so hungry. My stomach was hurting. Indian men and women were walking past me. I asked for food, but no one even looked at me.

I just sat on the ground and cried quietly. All I could do was think about home. What happened to my family? What had happened to John? What was going to happen to me?

Why were the Indians being so cruel? Back at the fort, I had heard about Indian raids on other families. I heard my grandpa say that the Indians killed lots of people. I also heard stories that Papa and the other men from the fort had raided Indian villages. Late at night, I'd hear them tell about killing Indian men, women, and even children.

Mama used to argue with Elder John and Papa all the time. "We've moved onto *their*

land," she'd say. "And we're eating *their* food. We need to make peace with them!"

This would make Papa angry. "It's *our* food, too!" he'd shout. "We'll never have peace with the Indians!"

"Why can't you just compromise?" Mama would ask, but no one would listen.

"Compromise," my mama always used to tell John and me. John and I used to get into plenty of fights, and Mama would always have to come break it up. "You've got to compromise," she'd say. "If everybody gives in just a little, you'll all come out with something you want!"

That's what I kept wondering as I sat on the ground in this strange place. I was alone and I was scared. Why can't the Indians and our families compromise now?

The Comanche camp Cynthia Ann lived in probably looked a lot like the one in this painting. Comanche women worked hard. One of their jobs was turning animal skins into clothes and rugs.

Chapter Three

BECOMING A COMANCHE

D ays went by. Sometimes I'd get hit for no reason. Every once in a while someone would throw me a piece of raw meat. Finally, I got so hungry that I'd try to eat it. It was so tough that I could barely chew it.

Groups of Indian children played nearby. They wore such strange clothes, not at all like ours. Mama would never have let us go out like that. "You must always look your best," she used to tell us. Oh, how I missed Mama.

One day a very tall man came up to me. He said something I couldn't understand. He pointed to a man and a woman who were standing next to him. They were smiling. The woman held her arms out toward me. The tall man was gesturing

me toward them. I realized that I was supposed to go with them.

At first I was scared. What were they going to do with me? Would they hurt me? They didn't hurt me. In fact, they treated me kindly. They gave me clothes, food, and a place to sleep. They taught me the ways of Comanche life. Also they gave me a new name. They called me Naduah.

I learned how to do chores such as gathering wood and watching younger children. I worked as hard as I could. Soon I was helping to cook and sewing buffalo skins together to make clothing. Little by little, I learned more and more Comanche words.

As the years went by, I became a real member of the Comanche tribe. I stopped thinking of my Parker family. Remembering them was painful and made me sad.

One day some white men came to our camp. This wasn't so unusual. Many times white men

would come to trade food, animals, and other things with our people. However, this time was different. They weren't pointing at food, blankets, or mules. They were pointing at me!

Someone told me to come forward. The white men carefully looked at me. They asked me questions, but I couldn't understand what they were saying. I now spoke only the language of the Comanche people. I could tell that these men wanted me to go with them. I did not want to go. I was a Comanche. Eventually, the white men left.

As I walked back to my family, one of our braves looked at me and nodded his head. His name was Peta Nocona. Soon I was to become his wife, and he was to become the chief of our tribe.

Hunting buffalo was an important part of Comanche life. Comanche men used spears as well as bows and arrows to kill the buffalo. Almost every part of the buffalo was used for food, clothes, or tools.

THE WIFE OF A CHIEF

Peta Nocona was a strong and brave warrior. He was my husband and my friend. Together we worked hard to keep our people safe and healthy. One day, another group of white traders came for me. They offered to give Peta Nocona anything he wanted. But he would not give me up. Even if he did, I would not have gone.

Over the years, Peta Nocona and I had three children. Our oldest was a boy whom we named Quanah. We then had another son named Pecos and a daughter named Topsannah.

Quanah was a strong and healthy child. He was willful, but he was always honest and fair. When the other children would fight, he would be the one to remind them to "compromise," just as I had

taught him. I believed he would be a great leader some day.

My sons could ride their horses better than anyone I had ever seen. They hunted with their father and other men, often for buffalo. Buffalo was a very important part of our lives. Without the buffalo, we would surely die. When the men brought back buffalo, the women would prepare the meat. We cut the meat into strips and dried it on racks. No part of the buffalo was wasted. We prepared the hides so they could be used for clothing, shoes, saddles, and shelter. We even used buffalo muscles like thread, to sew our clothing together.

In the spring, our people would have great celebrations. We would dress in our finest clothing. We would paint our faces and our bodies. We would dance and sing. It was always a time of much joy for all of us.

But along with our joy came sorrow too. Many of our people were dying from illnesses

we did not understand. Peta Nocona explained that these were illnesses that were brought by the white people.

Also, buffalo was becoming harder to find. Thousands of them were being killed by the white men. We sometimes had to travel great distances to find a herd to hunt.

Much fighting between our people and white soldiers began to happen. I heard Peta Nocona tell stories of how many of our people were being killed. Their homes were destroyed also.

Peta Nocona and other warriors went on raids and killed many settlers. The fighting went on and on. We often heard that there were soldiers nearby, ready to attack us. My husband was a great leader, and we had many brave warriors to protect us. Still, I was worried. Would we be safe if the white soldiers were to come?

Issac Parker spent close to twenty-five years looking for his niece, Cynthia Ann. Issac brought Cynthia Ann and her daughter to his home near Fort Worth, Texas.

Chapter Five

CAPTURED AGAIN!

O ne December day in 1860, my sons and I joined Peta Nocona on a buffalo hunt. Topsannah was riding with me. She was only two years old.

Suddenly, I heard someone yell. We looked up and saw a group of soldiers up on a hill. Minutes later, we were surrounded by soldiers riding toward us from every direction.

I saw Quanah and Pecos near their father. I held on tightly to Topsannah and rode as quickly as I could. I heard screaming and gunshots from all around, but I kept riding.

Suddenly, I was surrounded by soldiers. They aimed their guns at me. They looked at my face. Then they looked at Topsannah. I could not understand what they were saying, but they put their

guns down. One of them grabbed my horse, and they pulled us after them.

"My sons! My husband!" I cried. The soldiers could not understand me, but I continued to shout.

I was afraid for my sons. What if they came after me and the soldiers killed them? I could not risk their lives. Topsannah and I were brought to a camp where there were many white people. We were put in a tent. There were guards by the entrance.

The soldiers found someone who spoke my language. They told me that we would not be hurt. They told me that my family was coming to get me.

"My sons?" I asked. "My sons are coming to get me?"

"No," they answered. "Not your sons. Your real family is coming."

I was confused. What were they talking about? Who was my real family? Many days later, several white men came to see me. "I am

your Uncle Isaac," one of the men said to me. I did not know him. He was telling me about the family I had come from. "Your real family," he kept saying. "We all missed you, Cynthia Ann," he said.

Cynthia Ann—there was something about the sound of those words.

"Cynthia Ann?" I asked. Then I touched my chest. "Cynthia Ann!" I hit my chest harder. "Me Cynthia Ann!"

"Yes!" my uncle cried. "You are Cynthia Ann!"

My uncle took us back to where he lived. We met and stayed with several different members of my Parker family. Although they were all nice and treated us well, I still longed for my life with the Comanches. Several times we tried to escape, but we were always caught.

I cut my hair short, just like the Comanche women did as a sign of mourning. They took a photograph of me with Topsannah. I had never seen a photograph before. How strange it was!

As the years went by, I learned to speak their language again. I learned to do chores and to live the life of those around us. But I was never allowed to go searching for my sons and my husband.

In all those years, I did not talk about my life with the Comanches. I heard from a traveler that Quanah had become a chief, just as I knew he would. I'm sure he is a good leader. I don't know much more about my Comanche family, though.

I was told stories of how I was taken away as a child from Fort Parker. I was told that I was happy back then. But I know that I was happy as a Comanche wife and mother. That is the life that I think of as my own.

I am told that I should be happy now that I am among my "real people." However, I am lonely and sad. I keep all my thoughts to myself.

For more than twenty years, I was a Comanche. In my heart that is what I will always be.

GLOSSARY

brave (BRAYV) a Native American warrior

compromise (KOM-pruh-mize) to agree to accept something that's not exactly what you wanted

cultures (KUHL-churz) the ways of life, ideas, customs, and traditions of groups of people

frontier (fruhn-TIHR) the far edge of a country, where few people live

gesturing (JESS-tur-ihng) moving the head or hands to communicate a feeling or an idea

mourning (MORN-inhg) being very sad and grieving for someone who has died

pioneers (pye-un-NEERZ) people who explore unknown territories and settle there

raided (RAYD-ed) to have attacked a place suddenly and without warning

tomahawk (TOM-uh-hawk) a small ax once used by some North American Indians as a tool or weapon

warrior (WOR-ee-ur) a soldier, or someone who is experienced in fighting battles

willful (WIL-fuhl) deliberate

Primary Sources

To learn about the people and the events of the past, we can use many different sources. These sources include photographs, maps, letters, paintings, and diaries. For example, old photographs allow us to see what the people of the past looked like.

The photograph of Cynthia Ann Parker and her baby on page 30 was taken shortly after she was returned to the Parker family. By analyzing the photo, historians can see that Cynthia had cut her hair in the style of a Comanche woman in mourning.

Cynthia Ann's son Quanah is the subject of the photograph on page 31. We can compare and contrast this photo to photographs of Native Americans from other tribes. By doing so, we can identify how different tribes dressed.

Using sources such as these photographs help us understand the important people and events of the past.

This is one of the few photos of Cynthia Ann Parker. It was taken around 1861.

This picture of Cynthia Ann and her daughter, Topsannah, was taken soon after she was reunited with the Parker family.

Cynthia Ann's son, Quanah, grew up to be an important Comanche leader. He called himself Quanah Parker in honor of his mother.

Cynthia Ann Parker died in 1870. She was buried near Poyner, Texas. In 1910, Quanah Parker had Cynthia Ann's remains and those of her daughter, Topsannah, moved to a cemetery near his home in Cache, Oklahoma. The reburial ceremony (shown above) was held on December 4, 1910.